The Essential
BLOOD SUGAR DIET
MEDITERRANEAN
Recipe Book

A Quick Start Guide To Lose Weight, Reset Your Body And Live Longer With Mediterranean Diet Benefits

Over 80 Delicious Nutritious Calorie-Counted Mediterranean Style Recipes.

First published in 2018 by Erin Rose Publishing

Text and illustration copyright © 2018 Erin Rose Publishing

Design: Julie Anson

ISBN: 978-1-911492-50-4

A CIP record for this book is available from the British Library.

DISCLAIMER: This book is for informational purposes only and not intended as a substitute for the medical advice, diagnosis or treatment of a physician or qualified healthcare provider. The reader should consult a physician before undertaking a new health care regime and in all matters relating to his/her health, and particularly with respect to any symptoms that may require diagnosis or medical attention.

While every care has been taken in compiling the recipes for this book we cannot accept responsibility for any problems which arise as a result of preparing one of the recipes. The author and publisher disclaim responsibility for any adverse effects that may arise from the use or application of the recipes in this book. Some of the recipes in this book include nuts or other allergens. If you have an allergy it's important to avoid these.

CONTENTS

Recipes

INTRODUCTION

The Mediterranean Diet is hailed as being one of the best eating plans to improve blood sugar, diabetes, cholesterol, cardiovascular health and longevity. Insulin resistance is common which makes losing weight a struggle which is all too real. That's why a diet which is low in sugar and carbohydrates and rich in wonderfully nutritious fresh ingredients of the Mediterranean Diet are essential to boost weight loss and improve blood sugar.

Diet plays a vital role in longevity and wellbeing by preventing long term health issues. This book contains delicious Mediterranean style recipes which are low in carbohydrates to improve blood sugar and restore balance to your body.

The Mediterranean Diet has been scientifically proven time and time again to offer incredible health benefits, reducing the risk of health problems especially those associated with diabetes, obesity, heart disease and strokes. A vitally important key in losing weight and keeping it off is to maintain healthy blood sugar levels.

This **Quick Start Guide** contains clear, concise information on how to balance your blood sugar by using the principles of a low carbohydrate, Mediterranean diet to boost weight loss and improve your health. This recipe book contains delicious, calorie-counted recipes which are simple and easy while helping prevent hunger while you lose weight and improve your wellbeing. A winning combination for your health and your taste buds.

Are You Experiencing Blood Sugar Imbalance?

Blood sugar rises every time we eat and later falls as the short- term effect of our food wears off, creating a cycle of peaks and troughs of blood sugar levels throughout the day. This causes hunger and the desire to sustain sugar levels and energy. To prevent huge swings in your blood sugar it is best to avoid foods which cause a fast fix of energy i.e. sugar in all its forms and starchy carbohydrates. The effects of excess sugar and high insulin levels range from mild to severe and the emotional to the physical. It has been linked to:

- **Anxiety.**
- **Mood swings.**
- **Brain fog.**
- **Irritability.**
- **Lack of concentration.**
- **Depression and insomnia.**
- **Palpitations.**
- **Shakiness, fatigue and light headedness.**
- **Excess fat around the middle.**
- **Cravings for stimulants; coffee, sugar and alcohol.**
- **Difficulty losing weight.**
- **Pre-diabetes, type 2 diabetes and obesity**
- **Hypertension, high cholesterol, heart disease and strokes.**

> **Always consult with your doctor if you experience these symptoms to rule out other health conditions. Check with your doctor before embarking on any radical dietary changes, especially if you have a pre-existing medical condition.**

How to Get Started

Avoiding processed foods, sugar and refined carbohydrates is beneficial, especially if your diet includes sugar-rich sauces like sweet chilli, BBQ, ketchup and concentrated fruit juices or fast food containing hidden sugars. What if your diet is healthy and you're finding you still can't shift that extra weight? Setting your personal goal is a fundamental step, so decide what you want to achieve – is it to lose a few pounds or are you aiming for increased vitality and better health?

You can either remove starchy carbohydrates and sugar from your diet or if you want to maximise the benefits and focus on weight loss you can additionally restrict your calorie intake.

If you choose to limit your calorie intake, aim to consume no more than 1000 calories a day. Reducing your calorie intake will reduce excess fat from the midriff and improve weight loss. Plus getting rid of excess pounds will have an even greater beneficial effect on your blood sugar.

Fruit is packed with vitamins and nutrients, but it also contains fructose (fruit sugar). So while fruit is beneficial, sugar is not, so keep your intake low and opt for less sugary fruits like raspberries, blueberries and apples. Keep your fruit intake to no more than 2 pieces per day or less to begin with if you really struggle to balance your blood sugar or have sugar cravings. Tropical fruits, those exposed to more sunshine, contain higher fructose levels so mangoes, papayas and pineapples are best avoided completely.

Once you've decided how you want to approach your new health regime you can get started straight away. Familiarise yourself with what you can eat and remove tempting foods from your cupboards.

Adjust recipes and substitute ingredients to what you have in the fridge, for instance if a recipe asks for lettuce but you've run out, you can use a handful of fresh spinach leaves from the bag in the fridge. It'll cut down on waste and reduce any spoiling vegetable waste.

What Can I Eat?

FOODS TO AVOID:

Below is a list of the food categories detailing which foods to REDUCE or AVOID.

Carbohydrates

- Bread
- Biscuits
- Cereals
- Cakes
- Muesli
- Cookies
- Crackers

- Rice cakes
- Oat cakes
- Pasta
- Noodles
- Rice
- Millet
- Potatoes

Fats

- Vegetables oils such as corn and canola.
- Spreads and margarines which are low fat, contain trans fats or contain sugar.

Sugars

- Avoid products containing sugar, syrup, honey, chocolate, sweets and candy. Marinades and ready-made sauces such as sweet chilli sauces, ketchup, barbecue sauce, and any dressing containing sugar. Always read the labels as sugar is frequently added where you least expect it.
- Avoid dried fruit, like apricots, sultanas, raisins and figs.

Drinks

- Steer clear of beer, wine, spirits, cordials, fruit juices, milk, milk shakes, smoothies, fizzy drinks, hot chocolates, oat milk and rice milk.

What Can I Eat?

You CAN eat and enjoy the following foods.

Proteins

- All meat; beef, chicken, lamb, turkey, pork.

- Eggs

- Fresh fish such as tuna, haddock, cod, anchovies, salmon, trout, sardines, herring and sole. Shellfish such as prawns, mussels and crab.

- Tofu

- Nuts and nut butters

- Seeds

- Beans and pulses such as kidney beans, butter beans, chickpeas (garbanzo beans), pinto beans, cannellini beans, soy beans and lentils.

Fats

- Butter

- Avocados

- Coconut oil

- Olive Oil

- Ghee

- Nut butter

- Full-fat dairy produce; cheeses, Greek yogurt, sour cream, clotted cream, mascarpone, crème fraîche, fresh cream.

Fruit – Maximum 2 pieces of low sugar fruit per day

- Bananas
- Blackberries
- Blueberries
- Apples
- Apricots (fresh)
- Cherries
- Grapefruit

- Plums
- Kiwi
- Kumquat
- Lemons
- Limes
- Melon
- Oranges

- Peaches
- Pears
- Pomegranate
- Redcurrants
- Strawberries

Vegetables

- Root veg; such as parsnips, beetroots and carrots in moderation, as they have a higher carbohydrate content.
- Leeks
- Broccoli
- Cabbage
- Lettuce
- Celery
- Asparagus
- Artichokes
- Aubergine (eggplant)
- Bean sprouts
- Peppers (bell peppers)
- Broad beans
- Cabbage
- Runner beans
- Mushrooms
- Spinach
- Spring onions (scallions)
- Cucumber
- Courgette (zucchini)
- Radish
- Kale
- Cauliflower
- Pak Choi (Bok choy)
- Onions
- Brussels sprouts
- Rocket (arugula)
- Olives
- Watercress

Drinks

- Tea
- Coffee
- Green tea
- Water
- Almond Milk
- Soya Milk
- Double cream (heavy cream), coconut oil or butter can all be added to drinks.

Dressings & Condiments

Fresh herbs and spices such as; bay leaf, coriander (cilantro), chives, mint, thyme, rosemary, basil, parsley, oregano, cinnamon, cumin, mustard, dill, garlic, ginger, turmeric, paprika, cayenne pepper, chilli powder/ flakes, pepper and salt.

Healthy Low Carb Food Substitutions

One of the biggest challenges you will face is avoiding the hidden sugars and carbohydrates in certain foods, so read the labels to discover what you're really eating. Below is a list of low carbohydrate alternatives which can make great substitutes.

- Substitute rice for cauliflower 'rice' which can be adapted to suit your main course by adding herbs, spices or vegetables.

- Pasta is notoriously high in carbohydrates but a portion of courgette 'spaghetti' is a wonderful way of providing a filling and delicious alternative and it can be served alongside meat dishes and casseroles.

- Mashed potatoes are a traditional favourite but a low carbohydrate mashed cauliflower with a dollop of fresh butter, salt and pepper is a great alternative which kids love.

- Stevia is a good natural sweeter, which is a useful substitute for sugar and it has no known side effects associated with many artificial sweeteners.

- Avoid processed fats like margarines and hydrogenated vegetable oils. You can add healthy fats like coconut oil, olive oil, butter, nut butters and oils.

- Chocolate bars, sweets and candies can be swapped for good quality 80% cocoa chocolate or 100% cocoa powder or cacao nibs can be added to recipes. High cocoa content chocolate may have a small quantity of sugar in it (although less with higher cocoa content) but a small square of chocolate as a treat or recipe addition may be enough of a treat to help you keep eating healthily.

- Cocktails and liqueurs are often loaded with sugar so opt for dry wine instead.

- Swap crisps for vegetable crudités and dip.

- If you check out the ingredients list on processed soups you may realise they should be excluded from your diet due to excess carb/sugar content. Don't let preparation time put you off making your own soups. You can make a large batch and refrigerate or freeze them which will save you time in the long run.

- Be careful of flavoured yogurts – they have large amounts of sugar added. However plain or Greek yogurt is a great addition to your diet and you can get creative by adding, ground nuts, seeds, cocoa powder or a small amount of chopped fruit.

- Pancakes are not off the menu. You can swap ordinary white flour for almond or coconut flour. Or try our really simple recipe for banana pancakes which is so easy you'll wonder why you never thought of it before.

Recipes

BREAKFAST

Mozzarella Breakfast Muffins

Ingredients

200g (7oz) ham, chopped

75g (3oz) mozzarella cheese, grated (shredded)

8 large eggs, beaten

1 red pepper (bell pepper), finely chopped

1 small courgette (zucchini), finely chopped

MAKES 8

133 calories per serving

Method

Combine the beaten eggs with the ham, cheese, red pepper (bell pepper) and courgette (zucchini). Place paper cases inside an 8–hole muffin tin. Spoon the egg mixture into the cases. Transfer them to the oven and bake at 180C/360F for 20 minutes or until the eggs are completely set. These can be eaten hot or cold.

Baked Avocado Eggs

Ingredients

4 small eggs

2 large avocados, de-stoned and halved

1/4 teaspoon paprika

Sea salt

Freshly ground black pepper

SERVES 2

478
calories
per serving

Method

Preheat the oven to 220C/440F. Crack an egg into each of the avocado halves. You may need to remove a little of the avocado flesh to make room for the egg. Sprinkle with salt, pepper and paprika. Place them in an ovenproof dish and cook for 18-20 minutes until the eggs have set. Serve and eat straight away.

Easy Banana Pancakes

Ingredients

2 eggs

1 banana, mashed

2 teaspoons olive oil

SERVES
1

297
calories
per serving

Method

Whisk the eggs in a bowl and stir in the mashed banana. Combine them until the mixture is smooth. Heat the olive oil in a frying pan, add the pancake mixture and cook for around 2 minutes on each side or until the batter has set and the pancakes are golden. Serve and eat immediately. You can even add a little butter and a sprinkling of cinnamon on top.

Avocado & Chicken Omelette

Ingredients

25g (1oz) Cheddar cheese, grated (shredded)

50g (2oz) leftover chicken, chopped

2 eggs, beaten

Flesh of ½ avocado, chopped

1 teaspoon fresh basil

1 teaspoon olive oil

Freshly ground black pepper

**SERVES
1**

491
calories
per serving

Method

Heat the olive oil in a frying pan then pour in the beaten egg. While it begins to set sprinkle on the grated cheese, basil, chicken and chopped avocado. Cook until the eggs are completely set and the cheese has melted. Season with black pepper.

Olive, Tomato & Herb Frittata

Ingredients

50g (2oz) Cheddar cheese, grated (shredded)

75g (3oz) pitted black olives, halved

8 cherry tomatoes, halved

4 large eggs

1 tablespoon fresh parsley, chopped

1 teaspoon fresh basil, chopped

1 tablespoon olive oil

SERVES 2

381 calories per serving

Method

Break the eggs into a bowl and whisk them, then add in the parsley, basil, olives and tomatoes. Add in the cheese and stir it. Heat the oil in a small frying pan and pour in the egg mixture. Cook until the egg mixture completely sets. Place the frittata under a hot grill for 3 minutes to finish it off. Carefully remove it from the pan. Cut into slices and serve.

Mushroom & Bean Omelette

Ingredients

50g (2oz) tinned cannellini beans, drained

50g (2oz) mushrooms, chopped

2 eggs

1 red pepper (bell pepper), chopped

1 tablespoon olive oil

Dash of Tabasco sauce or a sprinkle of chilli powder

SERVES 1

341 calories per serving

Method

Heat the olive oil in a pan. Add the mushrooms, pepper (bell pepper) and beans. Cook for 3-4 minutes until the vegetables have softened. Remove them and set aside. Whisk the eggs in a bowl and pour them into the pan. Once the eggs begin to set, return the mushrooms, peppers and beans and spread them onto the eggs. Sprinkle with chilli or Tabasco sauce. Serve and eat straight away.

Tomato & Basil Scrambled Eggs

SERVES 2

252 calories per serving

Ingredients

400g (14oz) tinned chopped tomatoes

4 large eggs, beaten

1 small handful of fresh basil leaves, chopped

1 tablespoon olive oil

Sea salt

Freshly ground black pepper

Method

Heat the olive oil in a pan and add in the chopped tomatoes. Cook for around 10 minutes to reduce the tomato mixture down until the excess juice has evaporated. Slowly pour in the beaten egg, stirring constantly until the egg is completely cooked. Season and sprinkle with basil before serving.

Feta Cheese & Courgette Omelette

Ingredients

25g (1oz) feta cheese, crumbled

2 eggs

1 small courgette (zucchini), grated (shredded)

1 teaspoon fresh parsley, chopped

1 tablespoon olive oil

SERVES 1

337
calories
per serving

Method

Place the eggs in a bowl and whisk them. Stir in the cheese and courgette (zucchini). Heat the olive oil in a frying pan. Pour in the egg mixture and cook until it is set. Sprinkle with parsley and serve.

Quinoa & Red Pepper Scramble

Ingredients

100g (3½ oz) cooked quinoa

4 eggs, beaten

1 red pepper (bell pepper), chopped

¼ teaspoon paprika

1 tablespoon olive oil

Sea salt

Freshly ground black pepper

SERVES 2

261 calories per serving

Method

Heat the oil in a frying pan, and add red pepper (bell pepper) and paprika and cook for 3 minutes. Pour in the beaten eggs and stir continuously until they are almost firm. Add in th[e] quinoa and mix with the egg and pepper and warm it through. Season with salt and pepp[er] and serve.

Cheese & Ham Breakfast Peppers

Ingredients

25g (1oz) mozzarella cheese, grated (shredded)

2 red peppers (bell peppers), cut in half and de-seeded

2 slices ham cut in half

2 eggs, beaten

SERVES 2

160 calories per serving

Method

Place a slice of ham into each pepper half. Pour some of the beaten egg into each of the pepper halves. Place the mozzarella on top. Transfer the peppers to a baking sheet and cook in the oven at 190C/375F for 25 minutes or until the eggs have set.

Creamy Lime & Mint Smoothie

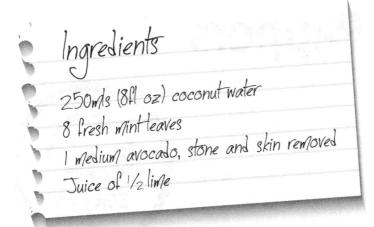

Ingredients

250mls (8fl oz) coconut water

8 fresh mint leaves

1 medium avocado, stone and skin removed

Juice of ½ lime

SERVES 1

323
calories
per serving

Method

Place the ingredients into a blender and blitz until smooth. You can add almond milk or some water if you like it thinner.

Apple & Grapefruit Smoothie

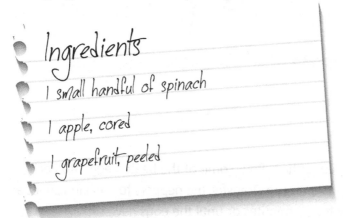

Ingredients

1 small handful of spinach

1 apple, cored

1 grapefruit, peeled

SERVES 1

105
calories
per serving

Method

Place all the ingredients into a blender with enough water to cover them and blitz until smoo

Cashew & Apricot Smoothie

Ingredients

- 25g (1oz) unsalted cashew nuts
- 1 small banana, peeled
- 1 apricot, stone removed
- 225mls (8fl oz) unsweetened almond milk

SERVES 1

249 calories per serving

Method

Place all of the ingredients into a blender and process until smooth. Serve and drink straight away.

Morning Coffee Smoothie

Ingredients

- 1 teaspoon instant coffee
- 1 banana, peeled
- 1 teaspoon 100% cocoa powder or cacao powder/nibs
- 175mls (6fl oz) almond milk

SERVES 1

141 calories per serving

Method

Place all of the ingredients into a blender and process until smooth. Serve with a few ice cubes

Carrot & Apple Smoothie

Ingredients

1 medium carrot, peeled
1 apple, cored
1/4 cucumber
Handful of fresh spinach

SERVES
1

102
calories
per serving

Method

Place all the ingredients into a blender and add around a cup of water. Blitz until smooth. You can add a little extra water if it's too thick.

Cherry & Melon Smoothie

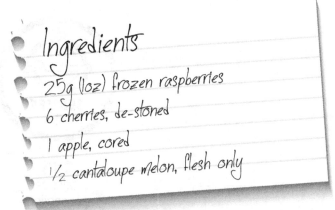

Ingredients

25g (1oz) frozen raspberries
6 cherries, de-stoned
1 apple, cored
1/2 cantaloupe melon, flesh only

SERVES
1

147
calories
per serving

Method

Place all the ingredients into a blender and add just enough water to cover the ingredients. Blitz until smooth. Serve and drink straight away.

LUNCH

Tomato & Basil Soup

Ingredients

2 x 400g (14oz) tins of chopped tomatoes

1 onion, peeled and chopped

1 small handful of fresh basil, chopped

600mls (1 pint) vegetable stock (broth)

125mls (4fl oz) double cream (heavy cream)

1 tablespoon olive oil

Sea salt

Freshly ground black pepper

SERVES 4

Method

Heat the oil in a saucepan, add the onion and cook for 5 minutes until the onion has soften
Add the tomatoes and stock (broth) and bring it to the boil. Reduce the heat and simmer for
minutes. Using a food processor and or hand blender blitz until smooth. Add in the basil, p
in the cream and warm it through. Season with salt and pepper. Serve and enjoy.

Fennel & Butterbean Soup

Ingredients

400g (14oz) butter beans
2 large fennel bulbs, chopped
1 carrot, chopped
1 onion, chopped
1 courgette (zucchini), chopped
1 clove of garlic, chopped
900mls (1 ½ pints) vegetable stock (broth)
Sea salt
Freshly ground black pepper

SERVES 4

127
calories
per serving

Method

Heat the vegetable stock (broth) in a large saucepan. Add in all of the vegetables but not the butterbeans just yet. Bring them to the boil, reduce the heat and simmer for 20 minutes. Add the butterbeans and stir until warmed through. Using a hand blender or food processor, process the soup until smooth. Season and serve.

Creamy Asparagus Soup

Ingredients

900g (2lbs) asparagus, tough end of stalk removed

2 tablespoons crème fraîche

1 onion, chopped

1 tablespoon olive oil

900mls (1½ pints) chicken stock (broth)

Sea salt

Freshly ground black pepper

SERVES 4

139 calories per serving

Method

Heat the oil in a large saucepan, add the onion and cook for 5 minutes. Break off the tough root end of the asparagus and roughly chop it. Place it in the saucepan and add the stock (broth). Bring it to the boil, reduce the heat and simmer for 20 minutes Using a food processor or hand blender process the soup until smooth and creamy. Stir in the crème fraîche. Season and serve.

Cream Of Mushroom Soup

Ingredients

450g (1lb) mushrooms, chopped

1 large leek, finely chopped

1 tablespoon cornflour (corn starch)

750mls (1¼ pints) vegetable stock (broth)

4 tablespoons crème fraîche

1 tablespoon olive oil

Sea salt

Freshly ground black pepper

SERVES 4

120 calories per serving

Method

Heat the olive oil in a saucepan. Add the leek and mushrooms and cook for 8 minutes or until the vegetables are soft. Sprinkle in the cornflour (corn starch) and stir. Pour in the stock (broth), bring it to the boil, cover and simmer for 20 minutes. Stir in the crème fraîche. Using a hand blender or food processor, blend the soup until smooth. Return to the heat if necessary. Season with salt and pepper just before serving.

Mozzarella Slices

Ingredients

300g (11oz) mozzarella cheese, grated (shredded)

4 eggs, beaten

3 cloves of garlic, crushed

2 teaspoons dried oregano

1 cauliflower (approx. 700g), grated (shredded)

Sea salt

Freshly ground black pepper

SERVES 8

139 calories per serving

Method

Place the cauliflower into a steamer and cook for 5 minutes. Place the cauliflower in a bowl and combine it with the mozzarella, eggs, oregano and garlic. Season with salt and pepper. Grease 2 baking sheets. Divide the mixture in half and place it on the baking sheet and press it into a flat rectangular shape. Preheat the oven to 220C/440F. Transfer the baking sheets to the oven and cook for for 20-25 minutes until golden. Slice and serve.

Feta & Spinach Slice

Ingredients

225g (8oz) feta cheese, grated (shredded)

125g (4oz) ground almonds

25g (1oz) fresh spinach leaves, chopped

2 eggs

1 onion, finely chopped

1 teaspoon baking powder

200mls (7fl oz) almond milk

SERVES 4

378 calories per serving

Method

Place the spinach into a saucepan, cover it with warm water, bring it to the boil and cook for 3 minutes. Drain it and set aside. Place the ground almonds in a bowl and add in the eggs, milk and baking powder and mix well. Add in the chopped onion, spinach and feta and combine the mixture. Spoon the mixture into a small ovenproof dish and smooth it out. Transfer it to the oven and bake at 190C/375F for 35 minutes. Cut into slices before serving.

Courgette Fritters

Ingredients

450g (1lb) courgettes (zucchinis), grated (shredded)

100g (3½ oz) Parmesan cheese

3 cloves of garlic, chopped

3 spring onions (scallions)

2 eggs

1 teaspoon dried mixed herbs

1 tablespoon olive oil

Sprinkling of salt

SERVES 4

204 calories per serving

Method

Place the grated (shredded) courgette (zucchini) into a colander and sprinkle with a little salt. Allow it to sit for 30 minutes then squeeze out any excess moisture. Place the eggs, Parmesan, spring onions (scallions), garlic and dried herbs into a bowl and mix well with the courgettes. Scoop out a spoonful of the mixture and shape it into patties. Heat the oil in a frying pan, add the patties and cook for 2 minutes, turn them over and cook for another 2 minutes. Serve warm.

Herby Tomato, Cannellini & Feta Salad

Ingredients

400g (14oz) tinned cannellini beans, drained
250g (9oz) cherry tomatoes, halved
75g (3oz) feta cheese, crumbled or diced
50g (2oz) fresh rocket (arugula) leaves
2 tablespoons fresh basil leaves, chopped
1 tablespoon fresh parsley, chopped
2 tablespoons olive oil
Juice of ½ lemon
Sea salt
Freshly ground black pepper

**SERVES
2**

364
calories
per serving

Method

Place all of the ingredients into a bowl and mix well. Season with salt and pepper.
Chill before serving.

Mozzarella & Aubergine Rolls

Ingredients

125g (4oz) mozzarella cheese

2 tomatoes, chopped

6 asparagus spears

1 aubergine (eggplant) cut into 6 lengthways slices

1 tablespoon fresh basil, chopped

1 tablespoon fresh chives, chopped

2 tablespoons olive oil

SERVES 2

336 calories per serving

Method

Heat the olive oil in a frying pan, add in the aubergine (eggplant) slices and cook for 2-3 minutes on each side. In the meantime, steam the asparagus for 5 minutes until it has softened. Place the aubergine slices onto plates and sprinkle some cheese, tomatoes and herbs onto each slice. Add an asparagus spear. Roll the aubergine slices up and secure it with a cocktail stick. Serve and enjoy.

Garlic Dough Balls

Ingredients

125g (4oz) almond flour (ground almonds/ almond meal)

75g (3oz) Parmesan cheese, grated (shredded)

50g (2oz) garlic butter

25g (1oz) mozzarella cheese, chopped

25g (1oz) butter, melted

1 egg

1 teaspoon pesto sauce

1 teaspoon garlic powder

MAKES
approx.**20**

88
calories
per serving

Method

Place all of the ingredients, apart from the garlic butter, into a bowl and combine them. Grease and line a baking tray. Scoop out a tablespoon of the mixture and roll it into a ball. Place it on a baking tray and repeat for the remaining mixture. Transfer it to the oven and bake at 180C/360F for around 20 minutes, or until golden. Spread some garlic butter onto each dough ball. Enjoy warm.

Prawn & Cannellini Avocados

SERVES 4

333 calories per serving

Ingredients

300g (11oz) tinned cannellini beans, drained

300g (11oz) cooked, shelled prawns

2 avocados, halved with stone removed

1 red pepper (bell pepper), finely chopped

2 cloves of garlic, crushed

1 tablespoon fresh coriander (cilantro)

1/2 teaspoon ground paprika

2 tablespoons olive oil

Juice of 1/2 lemon

Sea salt

Freshly ground black pepper

Method

Pour the lemon juice and olive oil into a bowl and mix well. Stir in the cannellini beans, prawns, red pepper (bell pepper), coriander (cilantro), garlic, paprika, salt and black pepper. Mix together until the ingredients are coated with the dressing. Serve the avocado halves onto plates and scoop the prawn mixture on top.

Pancetta & Kidney Bean Salad

Ingredients

400g (14oz) tin of cooked kidney beans,
100g (3½ oz) pancetta, diced
1 red pepper (bell pepper), finely chopped
3 tablespoons red wine vinegar
2 tablespoons fresh chives, chopped
1 tablespoon fresh basil, chopped
1 tablespoon olive oil
1 teaspoon smooth mustard
Sea salt
Freshly ground black pepper

**SERVES
2**

358
calories
per serving

Method

Heat a frying pan, add the pancetta and cook until crispy. Remove it and set it aside to cool. In a bowl, mix together the oil, vinegar, chives, basil and mustard. Stir in the red pepper (bell pepper), kidney beans and pancetta. Season with salt and pepper. Chill before serving.

Italian Lentil Salad

Ingredients

450g (1lb) green lentils
100g (3½ oz) hazelnuts, chopped
2 spring onions (scallions), chopped
1 cucumber, peeled and diced
1 red pepper (bell pepper), sliced
1 handful of fresh basil
Zest and juice of 1 lemon
100mls (3½ fl oz) olive oil
Sea salt
Freshly ground black pepper

SERVES 4

362 calories per serving

Method

Cook the lentils according to the instructions then allow them to cool. Pour the olive oil and lemon juice into a jug and combine them. Season with salt and pepper. Place all the ingredients for the salad into a bowl and pour on the olive oil and lemon juice.

Egg & Lentil Salad

Ingredients

200g (7oz) Puy lentils

4 eggs

4 tomatoes, deseeded and chopped

4 spring onions (scallions), finely chopped

2 tablespoons olive oil

2 tablespoons parsley

2 large handfuls of washed spinach leaves

1 clove of garlic

Juice and rind of 1 lemon

Sea salt

Freshly ground black pepper

**SERVES
4**

231
calories
per serving

Method

Place the lentils in a saucepan, cover them with water and bring them to the boil. Reduce the heat and cook for 20-25 minutes. Drain them once they are soft. Heat the olive oil in a saucepan, add the garlic and spring onions (scallions) and cook for 2 minutes. Stir in the tomatoes, lemon juice and rind. Cook for 2 minutes. Stir in the lentils and keep warm. In a pan of gently simmering water, poach the eggs until they are set but soft in the middle which should be 3-4 minutes. Scatter the spinach leaves onto plates, serve the lentils and top off with a poached egg. Season with salt and pepper. Sprinkle with parsley and serve.

Halloumi & Asparagus Salad

SERVES 4

257 calories per serving

Ingredients

450g (1lb) asparagus

250g (9oz) halloumi cheese, cut into slices

2 large handfuls of spinach leaves

1 tablespoon olive oil

Sea salt

Freshly ground black pepper

Method

Heat the olive oil in a frying pan and cook the asparagus for 4 minutes or until tender. Remove, set aside and keep warm. Place the halloumi in the frying pan and cook for 2 minutes on each side until golden. Serve the spinach leaves onto plates and add the asparagus and halloumi slices. Season with salt and pepper.

Chicken & Quinoa Salad

Ingredients

450g (1lb) chicken breasts, cooked and sliced
125g (4oz) quinoa, cooked
50g (2oz) fresh spinach leaves, chopped
8 spring onions (scallions), chopped
1 handful fresh coriander (cilantro), chopped
1 handful fresh parsley, chopped
2 tomatoes, diced
1 cucumber, peeled and diced
1 teaspoon ground turmeric
2 tablespoons olive oil
Juice of 1 lime
Sea salt
Freshly ground black pepper

SERVES 4

296
calories
per serving

Method

Combine all of the ingredients in a large bowl and mix well. Season with salt and pepper. Cover and place in the fridge for 20 minutes to chill before serving.

Greek Style Salad

Ingredients

350g (12oz) tomatoes, chopped
150g (5oz) feta cheese, crumbled
50g (2oz) pitted black olives, chopped
1 small onion, peeled and chopped
1 iceberg lettuce, finely chopped
1 cucumber, de-seeded and chopped

DRESSING:
3 tablespoons olive oil
Juice of 1 lemon
Sea salt
Freshly ground black pepper

SERVES 4

371
calories
per serving

Method

In a bowl, mix together the dressing ingredients. Place all of the salad ingredients into a bowl and add in the dressing. Toss the salad well before serving.

Tomato & Olive Salad

Ingredients

150g (5oz) cherry tomatoes, halved
75g (3oz) black olives, chopped
50g (2oz) capers
1 romaine lettuce, chopped
1 cucumber chopped
1 red pepper (bell pepper), sliced
1 onion, sliced
2 tablespoons red wine vinegar
1 tablespoon freshly squeezed lemon juice
1/2 teaspoon dried oregano
1/4 teaspoon dried basil
3 tablespoons olive oil
Sea salt
Freshly ground black pepper

SERVES 4

176 calories per serving

Method

Pour the vinegar into a large bowl and add in the olive oil, lemon juice, basil and oregano and mix well. Season with salt and pepper. Add the tomatoes, olives, capers, lettuce, cucumber, red pepper (bell pepper) and onion. Toss the salad ingredients in the dressing.

DINNER

Chicken Lasagne

Ingredients

450g (1lb) chicken either minced (ground) or finely diced

400g (14oz) ricotta cheese

300g (11oz) mozzarella cheese, grated (shredded)

2 x 400g (14oz) tins of chopped tomatoes

25g (1oz) Parmesan cheese, grated (shredded)

4 courgettes (zucchinis) sliced lengthways

3 tablespoons fresh basil, chopped

3 garlic cloves, peeled and chopped

1 onion, chopped

1 red pepper (bell pepper), chopped

1 teaspoon dried oregano

1 teaspoon dried mixed herbs

1 egg

1 tablespoon olive oil

Sea salt

SERVES 6

449 calories per serving

Method

Grease a baking sheet and lay the courgette (zucchini) slices on it. Season with salt, transfer it to the ove
and bake at 190C/375F for 15 minutes. In the meantime, heat the oil in a saucepan, add the onions, ga
and red pepper (bell pepper) and cook for 5 minutes. Add in the chicken and cook for 4 minutes. Stir
the tomatoes, basil and oregano and mixed herbs. Bring it to the boil, reduce the heat and simmer for 3
minutes. In a bowl combine the egg and ricotta cheese then set aside. When the chicken mixture is cool
spoon half of it into an ovenproof dish. Add a layer of the baked courgettes then spoon on half of the
ricotta mixture and a layer of mozzarella, repeat with the remaining mixture. Sprinkle Parmesan on top.
Transfer it to the oven and bake at 375F/180C for 40 minutes. Serve with a leafy green salad.

Lemon & Herb Lamb Chops

Ingredients

12 small lamb chops

1 tablespoon fresh thyme, chopped

1/2 tablespoon fresh rosemary leaves, chopped

4 tablespoons extra virgin olive oil

Juice of 1 lemon

SERVES 4

307
calories
per serving

Method

Pour the oil into a bowl and stir in the lemon juice, rosemary and thyme. Place the lamb chops in the mixture and allow it to marinate for at least 1 hour or overnight if you can. Transfer the chops to a hot grill (broiler) and cook for 5 minutes on either side or until the chops are cooked to your liking. Serve with a heap of salad or roast vegetables.

Steak & Cheese Lettuce Wraps

SERVES 4

344 calories per serving

Ingredients

450g (1lb) minced steak (ground steak)

100g (3½ oz) cheese, grated

2 tomatoes, sliced

2 tablespoons tomato purée (paste)

1 romaine lettuce, leaves washed and separated

1 teaspoon dried cumin

1 teaspoon paprika

½ teaspoon dried oregano

1 tablespoons olive oil

Method

Heat the olive oil in a frying pan, add the meat, cumin, paprika and oregano and cook for 10 minutes. Add in the tomato purée (paste) and cook for another 5 minutes until the meat is completely cooked. Lay out the lettuce leaves and spoon some meat into each one. Add the tomato slices and sprinkle with cheese. Serve and eat immediately. Your choice of toppings can be varied to include sour cream, guacamole, mushrooms, onions, chillies or red peppers

Bean & Quinoa Casserole

Ingredients

450g (1lb) black-eyed beans, drained

200g (7oz) frozen peas

100g (3½ oz) fresh spinach leaves

100g (3½ oz) quinoa

2 x 400g (14oz) tins of chopped tomatoes

2 cloves garlic, crushed

1 red onion, chopped

1 teaspoon cumin

1 teaspoon dried oregano

½ teaspoon chilli powder

125mls (4fl oz) water

1 tablespoon olive oil

**SERVES
4**

292
calories
per serving

Method

Heat the oil in a saucepan, add the onion and garlic and cook for 5 minutes. Transfer
to an ovenproof dish. Add in the quinoa, tomatoes, cumin, oregano and chilli powder.
Place the dish in the oven and cook at 180C/360F for 20 minutes. Stir in the beans, peas
and water. Cover with foil and cook for 20 minutes. Remove it from the oven, stir in the
spinach and allow it to wilt for a couple of minutes before serving.

Salmon, Butter Beans & Yogurt Dressing

Ingredients

- 400g (14oz) butter beans
- 125g (4oz) plain Greek yogurt (full-fat)
- 4 salmon fillets
- 3 cloves of garlic
- 1 red chilli, finely chopped
- 1/2 teaspoon paprika, plus extra for seasoning
- 1/2 teaspoon oregano
- 1 tablespoon olive oil
- Zest and juice 1/2 lemon
- Sea salt
- Freshly ground black pepper

SERVES 4

385 calories per serving

Method

Place the yogurt into a bowl and add in the lemon juice and paprika. Heat the oil in a pan, add the oregano, garlic and chilli and warm them for 2 minutes. Add in the butter beans and lemon zest and warm them through. Sprinkle the paprika over the salmon and season it with salt and pepper. Place the salmon fillets under a hot grill (broiler) and cook for around 8 minutes, or until completely cooked, turning half way through. Serve the salmon with the butter beans and a dollop of yogurt dressing.

Hunters Chicken

Ingredients

400g (14oz) broccoli florets

250g (8oz) tomato passata

125g (4oz) cheese, grated (shredded)

8 slices of bacon

4 chicken breasts

1 onion, chopped

2 tablespoons balsamic vinegar

1 tablespoon olive oil

SERVES 4

476 calories per serving

Method

Heat the oil in a frying pan, add the onion and cook for 5 minutes. Add the passata and balsamic and cook for 10 minutes to reduce the mixture. Place the chicken flat-side down on a lightly greased ovenproof dish and make an incision to make room for the sauce. Spoon the sauce into the incision. Wrap two slices of bacon around each chicken breast. Transfer the chicken to the oven and cook for 25 minutes. Scatter the cheese over the chicken breasts and return them to the oven for 5 minutes or until the cheese is bubbling. In the mean-time steam or boil the broccoli for 5 minutes. Serve the broccoli onto plates and add the chicken.

Mediterranean Fish Casserole

Ingredients

4 tuna steaks

2 red onions, chopped

2 stalks of celery

2 x 400g (2 x 14oz) tins of chopped tomatoes

2 cloves of garlic

1 tablespoon olive oil

1 lemon, thinly sliced

1 tablespoon tomato purée (paste)

2 tablespoons fresh oregano, chopped

Sea salt

Freshly ground black pepper

SERVES 4

229 calories per serving

Method

Heat the oil in a saucepan and add the celery, garlic and onions and fry for 5 minutes until the vegetables have softened. Add in the tinned tomatoes, oregano, tomato puree (paste) and lemon slices. Bring to the boil and simmer for 5 minutes, stirring occassionally. Season with salt and pepper. Place the fish in the tomato mixture. Simmer gently for 12-14 minutes until the fish is cooked. Serve the fish onto plates and pour the sauce on top. Garnish with a little oregano.

Tomato & Herb Stuffed Chicken

Ingredients

450g (1lb) chicken breasts

75g (3oz) black olives, finely chopped

50g (2oz) butter, softened

6 sundried tomatoes, finely chopped

3 cloves of garlic, crushed

1 tablespoon capers

1 teaspoon dried oregano

1 teaspoon dried basil

Sea salt

Freshly ground black pepper

SERVES 4

333
calories
per serving

Method

Place the olives, tomatoes, garlic, dried herbs and capers into a bowl and stir. Add in the softened butter and capers and mix well. Make an incision in each chicken breast to make a pocket for the butter mixture. Spoon the mixture inside each of the chicken breasts. Season with salt and pepper and wrap each one in tin foil. Transfer them to the oven and cook at 190C/375F for 25 minutes.

Lemon & Coriander (Cilantro) Chicken

Ingredients

- 450g (1lb) chicken breasts
- 1 onion, finely chopped
- 3 cloves of garlic, crushed
- 2 lemons, sliced and pips removed
- 1 teaspoon ground coriander
- 1 teaspoon ground ginger
- 1 teaspoon ground cumin
- 1 teaspoon ground turmeric
- 1 tablespoon olive oil
- 600mls (1 pint) chicken stock (broth)
- 125g (4oz) pitted green olives
- Handful of fresh coriander (cilantro) finely chopped

SERVES 4

278 calories per serving

Method

Heat the oil in a saucepan, add the onion and cook for 5 minutes until softened. Add the garlic, cumin, turmeric, ginger and ground coriander (cilantro) and cook for 1 minute. Add the chicken and brown it. Add the slices of lemon and chicken stock (broth). Bring it to the boil, reduce the heat and simmer for 30 minutes. Stir in the fresh coriander (cilantro) and olives. Warm the olives through and then serve.

Golden Cauliflower 'Rice'

Ingredients

1 head of cauliflower, approx. 700g (1½ lb)

1 tablespoon olive oil

Sea salt

Freshly ground black pepper

SERVES 4

81 calories per serving

Method

Place the cauliflower into a food processor and chop until fine, similar to rice. Heat the olive oil in a frying pan, stir in the cauliflower and cook for 5-6 minutes or until softened. Season with salt and pepper. Serve with meat or vegetable dishes as a tasty alternative to rice.

Mediterranean Fried 'Rice'

Ingredients

200g (7oz) mushrooms, finely chopped

6 spring onions (scallions), finely chopped

1 head of cauliflower, approx. 700g (1½ lb) broken into florets

1 red pepper (bell pepper), peeled and finely chopped

1 onion, finely chopped

1 large egg, beaten

2 tablespoons olive oil

2 tablespoons soy sauce

Sea salt

Freshly ground black pepper

SERVES 4

149 calories per serving

Method

Place the cauliflower pieces into a food processor and chop until it becomes grain-like. In a bowl mix together the egg with a tablespoon of soy sauce. Heat a tablespoon of oil in a large frying pan or wok. Add the egg mixture and scramble it for a few minutes then remove it and set aside. Heat the remaining olive oil and add in the red onion and cook for 5 minutes. Add in all the remaining vegetables and cook them for around 5 minutes until they soften. Stir in the remaining soy sauce. Add the cooked egg mixture and stir well. Season with salt and pepper. Serve instead of traditional fried rice.

Paprika Chicken & Butternut Squash

Ingredients

125g (4oz) olives, stones removed and halved

8 chicken drumsticks

8 cherry tomatoes

2 large courgettes (zucchinis), cut into chunks

1 teaspoon dried oregano

1 butternut squash, peeled and cut into chunks

1 large handful of fresh spinach leaves

1 teaspoon paprika

1/2 teaspoon cumin

2 tablespoons olive oil

SERVES 4

429
calories
per serving

Method

Preheat the oven to 200C/400F. Pour the oil into a roasting tin with the paprika, oregano and cumin and stir. Add in the squash and chicken drumsticks and coat them in the mixture. Transfer the roasting tin to the oven and cook for 40 minutes. Add in the tomatoes, olives, courgettes (zucchini) and spinach leaves and coat them in the oil. Return it to the oven and cook for 10 minutes.

Parmesan Chicken & Asparagus

Ingredients

- 350g (12oz) asparagus spears, trimmed
- 25g (1oz) Parmesan cheese, grated
- 4 chicken breasts
- 4 cloves of garlic, chopped
- 2 red peppers (bell peppers), deseeded and chopped
- 2 tomatoes, chopped
- 2 tablespoons fresh basil, chopped
- 2 tablespoons fresh parsley, chopped
- 2 tablespoons fresh tarragon, chopped
- 1 tablespoon capers, drained
- Zest of 1 lemon
- 2 tablespoons olive oil

SERVES 4

176 calories per serving

Method

Preheat the oven to 200C/400F. Place the herbs, garlic, capers and olive oil into a food processor and blitz to combine them. Combine the mixture with the lemon zest and parmesan. Spread the topping onto the chicken breasts. Add the chicken to a roasting tin. Place it in the oven and cook for 10 minutes. Add in the asparagus, red peppers (bell peppers) and tomatoes. Return it to the oven and cook for 10-15 minutes or until the vegetables have softened and the chicken is completely cooked.

Salmon Kebabs

Ingredients

8 button mushrooms

8 pitted black olives

4 salmon fillets

2 tablespoons fresh parsley, chopped

Juice and rind of 1 lemon

3 tablespoons olive oil

**SERVES
4**

385
calories
per serving

Method

Cut the salmon into chunks and place them in a bowl. Squeeze in the lemon juice and add the rind, olive oil and parsley and coat the salmon chunks thoroughly. Add the mushrooms and coat them in the dressing too. Thread the fish, olives and mushrooms onto skewers. Place them under a hot grill (broiler) and cook for 4-5 minutes turning occasionally. Serve the kebabs and drizzle them with the remaining dressing.

Spinach & Cheese Stuffed Chicken

Ingredients

4 chicken breasts

4 tablespoons cream cheese

25g (1oz) spinach leaves

1 tablespoon fresh parsley

1 tablespoon fresh chives

SERVES 4

192 calories per serving

Method

In a bowl, combine the cream cheese, spinach and herbs until it's well mixed. Carefully make an incision on the underside of the chicken breast, wide enough to contain some cheese mixture. Spoon some of the mixture into the incision and press the chicken back together. Repeat for the remaining mixture. Place the stuffed chicken in an ovenproof dish. Transfer to the oven and bake at 180C/360F for around 30 minutes or until the chicken is completely cooked. Serve with a large green leafy salad. Enjoy.

Tuna & Lentil Bake

Ingredients

200g (7oz) tinned tuna in brine, drained
250g (9oz) lentils
50g (2oz) cheese, grated (shredded)
1 onion, peeled and finely chopped
1 carrot, peeled and finely chopped
1 handful of fresh parsley, chopped
1 handful of fresh chives, chopped
450mls (15fl oz) vegetable stock (broth)
1 tablespoon olive oil

**SERVES
4**

448
calories
per serving

Method

Preheat the oven to 200C/400F. Pour the stock (broth) into a saucepan, add the lentils and cook for 12 minutes. Drizzle the olive oil into an ovenproof dish. Scatter the lentils into the dish and add the flaked tuna, onion, carrot and herbs and mix well. Sprinkle the cheese over the top. Transfer it to the oven and cook for around 20 minutes. Serve and eat straight away.

Coriander & Coconut Baked Salmon

Ingredients

4 salmon fillets,

120mls (4fl oz) coconut milk

1 large handful of coriander (cilantro) leaves

2.5cm (1 inch) chunk of ginger

1 teaspoon garam masala

3 cloves of garlic, crushed

1 chilli pepper, de-seeded and chopped

**SERVES
4**

228
calories
per serving

Method

Pour the coconut milk into a blender and add in the ginger, garam masala, garlic, chilli and coriander (cilantro). Process until smooth. Place the salmon fillets in an ovenproof dish and pour the coconut milk over the fish. Transfer it to the oven and bake at 220C/440F for 15-20 minutes until the fish is cooked through.

Sea Bass & Ratatouille

Ingredients

4 skinless sea bass fillets
4 cloves of garlic, chopped
1 yellow pepper (bell pepper), chopped
1 red pepper (bell pepper), chopped
1 large courgette (zucchini), chopped
1 aubergine (eggplant), chopped
1 teaspoon dried mixed herbs
1 tablespoon olive oil
1 large handful of fresh basil leaves, chopped
Sea salt
Freshly ground black pepper

**SERVES
4**

195
calories
per serving

Method

Place the courgette (zucchini) aubergine (eggplant), peppers, garlic, mixed herbs and oil, into an ovenproof roasting dish and toss them well. Season with salt and pepper. Transfer it to the oven and cook at 200C/400F for 25 minutes. Add in half of the fresh basil and stir the vegetables. Place the fish on top of the vegetables. Return it to the oven and cook for 10-12 minutes or until the fish is completely cooked and flakes off. Sprinkle the remaining basil on top and serve.

Roast Courgettes & Olives

Ingredients

10 pitted black olives, chopped

4 medium courgettes (zucchinis), thickly sliced lengthways

2 tablespoons tomato purée (paste)

1 clove of garlic, crushed

1 teaspoon mixed herbs

2 tablespoons olive oil

Sea salt

Freshly ground black pepper

SERVES 4

107 calories per serving

Method

In a bowl, combine the olive oil, garlic, tomato purée (paste) and mixed herbs. Place the courgette (zucchini) slices in an ovenproof dish and spread the oil mixture over the slices. Sprinkle with olives and season with salt and pepper. Transfer them to an oven, preheated to 200C/400F and cook for 15 minutes.

Mini Cauliflower Pizza Bases

Ingredients

- 350g (12 oz) mozzarella cheese, grated (shredded)
- 200g (7oz) passata/ tomato sauce
- 2 eggs
- 1 head of cauliflower approx. 700g (1½lb), grated (shredded)
- 1 teaspoon dried oregano
- 1 teaspoon dried basil
- 1 teaspoon garlic powder
- 1 tomato, sliced
- Handful of fresh basil leaves, chopped

**SERVES
6**

219
calories
per serving

Method

Steam the grated (shredded) cauliflower for 5 minutes then allow it to cool. Place the cooked cauliflower in a bowl and add the eggs, half the cheese, all of the dried herbs and garlic and mix everything together really well. Grease two baking sheets. Divide the mixture into 12 and roll it into balls. Place them on a baking sheet and press them down until are flat and round mini pizza bases. Transfer them to the oven and bake at 220C/440F for 12 minutes until lightly golden. Top each pizza base with a little passata, the remaining mozzarella and tomato and fresh basil. Place the pizzas under a grill (broiler) and cook for 4-5 minutes or until the cheese has melted. Enjoy.

Mediterranean Cod

Ingredients

400g (14oz) tin of chopped tomatoes

75g (3oz) pitted black olives, sliced

4 cod fillets

1 onion, chopped

2 cloves of garlic, crushed

2 tablespoons olive oil

100mls (3½fl oz) vegetable or chicken stock (broth)

A small handful of fresh parsley

SERVES 4

223 calories per serving

Method

Heat the oil in a frying pan, add the onions and garlic and cook for 5 minutes. Add in chopped tomatoes, parsley, olives and stock. Bring it to the boil and simmer for 5 minutes. Add the cod fillets in the sauce and simmer gently for 5-6 minutes or until the fish is white and thoroughly cooked.

Pork Steaks, Peppers & Beans

Ingredients

400g (14oz) cannellini beans, drained

8 pork steaks

4 tablespoons fresh parsley, chopped

2 red peppers (bell peppers)

1 onion, chopped

1 tablespoon red wine vinegar

1 tablespoon olive oil

Sea salt

Freshly ground black pepper

SERVES 4

460
calories
per serving

Method

Season the pork steaks with salt and pepper. Heat the olive oil in a frying pan, add the pork and cook for around 3 minutes on each side. Remove them, set aside and keep them warm. Add the peppers (bell peppers) and onion to the pan and cook for 5 minutes until the vegetables have softened. Add the parsley, vinegar and beans and warm them thoroughly. Serve the pork steaks and spoon the vegetables over the top. Enjoy.

Fresh Basil, Mozzarella & Tomato Chicken

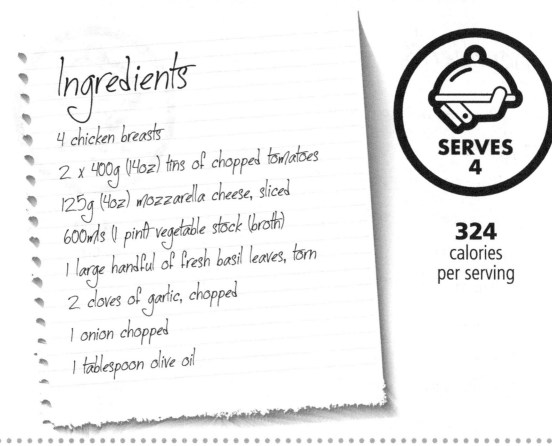

Ingredients

- 4 chicken breasts
- 2 x 400g (14oz) tins of chopped tomatoes
- 125g (4oz) mozzarella cheese, sliced
- 600mls (1 pint) vegetable stock (broth)
- 1 large handful of fresh basil leaves, torn
- 2 cloves of garlic, chopped
- 1 onion chopped
- 1 tablespoon olive oil

SERVES 4

324 calories per serving

Method

Heat the olive oil in a frying pan, add the onion and garlic and cook for 5 minutes or until softened. Add the chopped tomatoes and stock (broth). Add in the basil leaves, bring it to the boil, reduce the heat and simmer for 5 minutes. Place the chicken in an ovenproof dish. Cover the chicken with the sauce and add slices of mozzarella to the dish on top of the chicken. Transfer it to the oven and cook at 190C/375F for around 20 minutes or until the chicken is completely cooked. Serve with a leafy green salad.

Salmon & Olive Bake

Ingredients

450g (1lb) courgettes (zucchinis), roughly chopped

2 x 400g (2x14oz) tins chopped tomatoes

100g (3½ oz) black olives in brine, drained

4 salmon fillets

1 onion, roughly chopped

2 tablespoons fresh basil

2 tablespoons fresh parsley

1 tablespoon olive oil

**SERVES
4**

453
calories
per serving

Method

Preheat the oven to 200C/400F. Add the olive oil, onion, courgette (zucchini), tinned tomatoes, olives, basil and parsley to the roasting tin and cook in the oven for 10 minutes. Lay the salmon fillets on top. Return the roasting tin to the oven and cook for 12-15 minutes or until the salmon is completely cooked. Serve and enjoy!

Baked Eggs & Vegetables

Ingredients

4 eggs

1 red pepper (bell pepper), chopped

1 green pepper (bell pepper), chopped

1 large aubergine (eggplant), chopped

1 bulb of fennel, chopped

1 onion, chopped

3 cloves of garlic, chopped

1 handful of fresh basil

2 tablespoons olive oil

SERVES 4

174 calories per serving

Method

Place all the vegetables, garlic and basil in a large ovenproof dish. Pour in the olive oil and toss the vegetables. Transfer it to the oven and cook at 200C/400F for 20 minutes. Make 4 round indentations in the vegetables and crack an egg into each space. Place the dish back into the oven and cook for 10 minutes. Serve and eat immediately.

Chilli Chicken Skewers & Roast Cauliflower

Ingredients

450g (1lb) chicken breast, diced

12 cherry tomatoes

1 large cauliflower

1 onion, peeled and chopped

1 teaspoon smoked paprika

1/2 teaspoon mild chilli powder

2 tablespoons olive oil

Sea salt

Freshly ground black pepper

SERVES 4

292
calories
per serving

Method

Preheat the oven to 180C/360F. Place the chicken into a large bowl and add the chilli and smoked paprika and a tablespoon of olive oil. Coat the chicken completely in the mixture. Add a tablespoon of olive oil to a large roasting tin. Cut the cauliflower into slices. Scatter them in the roasting tin, together with the onion and coat them in olive oil. Thread the chicken chunks, onto skewers, alternating them with the tomatoes. Lay the chicken skewers in top of the cauliflower and season with salt and pepper. Transfer the roasting tin to the oven and cook for 25-30 minutes or until the chicken is completely cooked and the cauliflower is tender. Serve and eat straight away.

Cauliflower Mash

Ingredients

1 large head of cauliflower,
approx. 700g (1½lb), broken into florets

75g (3oz) Cheddar cheese, grated (shredded)

75g (3oz) crème fraîche

1 clove of garlic, crushed

**SERVES
6**

107
calories
per serving

Method

Place the cauliflower in a steamer along with the garlic and cook until the cauliflower
has softened. Drain it and allow it to cool just a little. Transfer it to a food processor and
process until smooth. Stir in the crème fraîche and cheese and mix it well. Serve instead
of traditional mashed potatoes.

Herby Quinoa & Bean Traybake

Ingredients

- 2 x 400g (2 x 14oz) tins of chopped tomatoes
- 400g (14oz) tin of black beans, drained and rinsed
- 175g (6oz) quinoa
- 125g (4oz) tinned sweetcorn
- 2 cloves of garlic, finely chopped
- 2 red peppers (bell pepper), deseeded and finely chopped
- 1 courgette (zucchini), diced
- 1 onion, finely chopped
- 1 teaspoon dried oregano
- 1 teaspoon paprika
- 1 large handful of fresh basil leaves, chopped
- 2 tablespoons olive oil
- Juice of ½ lime
- 400mls (14fl oz) vegetable stock (broth)

SERVES 6

328 calories per serving

Method

Preheat the oven to 180C/360F. Cook the quinoa in the vegetable stock (broth) according to the timing in the instructions and then drain it. Place the onion, peppers, garlic, courgette (zucchini), beans, tomatoes and sweetcorn in a bowl and mix well. Add in the spices, oil and lime juice to the mixture. Transfer it in to an ovenproof dish or roasting tin. Add in the quinoa and mix well. Cook it in the oven for 40 minutes. Add in the fresh herbs and stir them throughout. Serve with a heap of green salad.

Mustard & Garlic Prawns

Ingredients

450g (1lb) large fresh uncooked prawns, peeled

125g (4oz) butter

2 red peppers (bell peppers), sliced

2 tablespoons Dijon mustard

Juice of half a lemon

2 cloves of garlic, chopped

Sea salt

Freshly ground black pepper

SERVES 4

331 calories per serving

Method

Place the prawns in an ovenproof dish and scatter the red peppers (bell peppers) into the dish. Heat the butter in a small saucepan and stir in the mustard, garlic and lemon juice. Warm the mixture until the butter has melted. Pour the butter over the prawns and peppers. Season with salt and pepper. Transfer to the oven and bake at 220C/425F for 15 minutes or until the prawns are pink and completely cooked.

Halloumi & Butternut Squash Traybake

Ingredients

600g (1lb 5oz) butternut squash, peeled and diced

350g (1lb) halloumi cheese, thickly sliced

25g (1oz) pine nuts

8 cherry tomatoes, halved

3 cloves of garlic, chopped

2 onions, peeled and chopped

1 yellow pepper (bell pepper), deseeded and chopped

1 red pepper (bell pepper), deseeded and chopped

1 handful of fresh basil, chopped

1 handful of fresh parsley, chopped

2 teaspoons paprika

1 tablespoon olive oil

**SERVES
4**

488
calories
per serving

Method

Preheat the oven to 200C/400F. Scatter the butternut squash, tomatoes, onions, peppers and garlic into a roasting tin. Coat them in paprika and olive oil. Toss them well in the mixture. Lay the halloumi on top of the vegetables. Transfer it to the oven and cook for 25 minutes or until the sweet potatoes are tender and the halloumi is golden. Add in the parsley, basil and pine nuts and serve.

Marinated Pork Chops

Ingredients

- 4 pork chops
- 4 cloves garlic, minced
- 2 teaspoons ground coriander (cilantro)
- 1/2 teaspoon ground black pepper
- 75mls (2fl oz) soy sauce
- 2 tablespoons olive oil
- 1 tablespoon balsamic vinegar
- Juice of 1/2 lemon

SERVES 4

320 calories per serving

Method

Place the garlic, balsamic, soy sauce, lemon juice, olive oil, coriander (cilantro) and pepper in a bowl and mix well. Add the pork chops to the bowl and coat them thoroughly in the mixture. Cover and refrigerate them for at least 30 minutes, or overnight if you can. When they are sufficiently marinated, heat a frying pan and add the chops together with all of the marinade. Cook for 5 minutes on each side, or until the chops are thoroughly cooked. Serve with a heap of green salad and cauliflower rice.

Slow Cooked Chicken

Ingredients

1 large whole chicken, approx. 1.8kg (4lb)

2 onions, peeled and halved

1 teaspoon smoked paprika

Sea salt

Freshly ground black pepper

SERVES 6

423 calories per serving

Method

Sprinkle the smoked paprika onto the chicken and season with salt and pepper. Place the onions inside the chicken. Transfer it to a slow cooker and cook on high for 6-8 hours or until the chicken is completely cooked and very tender. Serve the chicken with the juices spooned over the top and a heap of fresh vegetables.

Tomato, Pomegranate & Feta Bake

Ingredients

450g (1lb) cherry tomatoes, halved

75g (3oz) pomegranate seeds

2 blocks of feta cheese, halved widthways

2 teaspoons ground coriander

½ teaspoon chilli powder

1 tablespoon olive oil

1 handful of fresh parsley, chopped

SERVES 4

328 calories per serving

Method

Scatter the tomatoes into an oven proof dish, and sprinkle with coriander (cilantro) and chilli powder. Transfer it to the oven and cook at 220C/440F for 15 minutes. Lay the feta on top of the tomato mixture, drizzle with the olive oil. Return it to the oven and continue cooking for 7-10 minutes or until the feta is golden. Sprinkle with the pomegranate seeds and parsley. Serve with a heap of green salad.

Low Carb Cottage Pie

Ingredients

450g (1lb) steak mince (ground steak)

400g (14oz) tinned chopped tomatoes

1 carrot, peeled and finely chopped

1 cauliflower (approx. 700g (1½lb) broken into florets

1 leek, trimmed and finely chopped

1 onion, chopped

1 tablespoon soy sauce

1 tablespoon tomato purée (paste)

1 tablespoon olive oil

1 small handful fresh parsley, chopped

300mls (½ pint) beef stock (broth)

SERVES 4

370 calories per serving

Method

Heat the oil in a saucepan, add the mince and cook for 3 minutes. Add in the carrot and onion and cook for 5 minutes. Add in the tomatoes, tomato purée, soy sauce, parsley and stock (broth). Bring it to the boil, reduce the heat and simmer for 30 minutes. In the meantime, boil the cauliflower until tender then drain it. Mash until soft. Fry the leeks in a pan until they become soft. Combine the leeks with the mashed cauliflower. Transfer the meat to an ovenproof dish and spoon the cauliflower mixture on top. Place the dish in the oven at 200C/400F for around 30 minutes or golden on top.

Prawn & Chickpea Oven Traybake

Ingredients

400g (14oz) tin of chopped tomatoes

400g (14oz) tin of chickpeas (garbanzo beans), drained

300g (10oz), prawns (shrimps), peeled

2 cloves of garlic, chopped

1 teaspoon paprika

3 tablespoons olive oil

1 small handful fresh parsley, chopped

SERVES 4

235 calories per serving

Method

Heat the oven to 190C/380F. Scatter the chickpeas (garbanzo beans), tomatoes, garlic and paprika into an oven proof dish. Add in the olive oil and mix well. Transfer it to the oven and cook for 10 minutes. Scatter the prawns into the dish, return it to the oven and cook for around 10 minutes or until the prawns are pink and completely cooked through. Sprinkle with parsley. Serve with crusty bread, rice or salad.

Lamb Shank Casserole

Ingredients

2 lamb shanks

4 large mushrooms, chopped

3 carrots, chopped

3 cloves of garlic, crushed

2 large tomatoes, chopped

1 onion, finely chopped

2 tablespoons tomato purée (paste)

2 large sprigs of rosemary

1 bouquet garni

1/2 bulb of fennel, chopped

750ml (1/2 pints) beef vegetable stock (broth)

2 tablespoons olive oil

**SERVES
2**

432
calories
per serving

Method

Heat the oil in a large saucepan and add the lamb, turning occasionally until it is brown all over. Transfer the lamb to a bowl and set aside. Add the onion, fennel, mushrooms, carrots and garlic to the saucepan and cook for 5 minutes. Return the lamb to the saucepan and add in the stock (broth), tomatoes, tomato purée (paste), rosemary, and bouquet garni. Transfer to an oven-proof dish, cover and cook in the oven at 200C/400F for 2 hours. Check half way through cooking and add extra stock (broth) or water if necessary. Remove the bouquet garni. Serve and enjoy.

Spicy Meatballs & Minty Yogurt Dip

Ingredients

450g (1lb) minced turkey (or beef)

50g (2oz) ground almonds

3 tablespoons harissa paste

1 tablespoon tomato purée (paste)

2 garlic cloves, crushed

Juice of 1 lemon

1 egg

2 tablespoons olive oil

FOR THE DIP:

200g (7oz) plain yogurt (unflavoured)

12 mint leaves, finely chopped

SERVES 4

346 calories per serving

Method

In a bowl, combine the turkey with 2 tablespoons of harissa paste, the almonds, garlic, lemon juice and egg and mix really well. Scoop portions of the mixture out with a spoon and shape into balls. Cover and refrigerate for 40 minutes. Heat the oil in a frying pan, add a tablespoon of harissa paste and tomato purée (paste) and stir. Add the meatballs and cook for 7-8 minutes, turning occasionally until thoroughly cooked. In the meantime, combine the yogurt and mint and mix well. Skewer each meatball with a cocktail stick and serve ready to be dipped in the yogurt. Enjoy.

Cannellini & Vegetable Bake

Ingredients

400g (14oz) cannellini beans

150g (5oz) cherry tomatoes, halved

150g (5oz) button mushrooms

3 cloves of garlic, peeled and chopped

3 celery stalks, chopped

3 medium carrots, peeled and roughly chopped

1 large onion, peeled and chopped

1 butternut squash, peeled and cut into chunks

1 courgette (zucchini), chopped

1 teaspoon dried thyme

1 teaspoon dried oregano

1 large handful of fresh basil

A small handful of fresh parsley, chopped

2 tablespoons olive oil

Sea salt

Freshly ground black pepper

SERVES 4

295 calories per serving

Method

Place the beans and vegetables into a roasting tin. Sprinkle in the dried herbs, garlic and olive oil and toss all of the ingredients together. Season with salt and pepper. Transfer them to an oven, preheated to 180C/360F and cook for 30-40 minutes or until all of the vegetables are softened. Scatter in the fresh parsley just before serving.

DESSERTS

Nutty Chocolates

Ingredients

125g (4oz) almonds, chopped

125g (4oz) walnuts, chopped

50g (2oz) desiccated (shredded) coconut

50g (2oz) coconut oil

2 eggs, whisked

2 tablespoons 100% cocoa powder (or cacao nibs)

2 tablespoons tahini (sesame) paste

2 tablespoons peanut butter

1 tablespoon sunflower seeds

1 teaspoon ground cinnamon

1 tablespoon stevia

MAKES 24

128 calories per serving

Method

Place all the ingredients into a bowl or a food processor and mix it well, keeping the nuts a nice chunky texture. Spoon the mixture into small paper baking cases. Transfer them to the oven and bake at 180C/360F for 20 minutes. Allow them to cool then store them in an airtight container.

Chocolate Orange Cheesecake

Ingredients

800g (1½ lb) mascarpone cheese

4 medium eggs, beaten

3 tablespoons 100% cocoa powder

1 tablespoon orange juice

1 teaspoon freshly grated orange zest

1-2 tablespoon stevia sweetener (or to taste)

SERVES 10

391
calories
per serving

Method

Place the mascarpone cheese into a large bowl and beat it until soft and smooth. Stir in the beaten eggs, orange juice, orange zest, cocoa powder and stevia and mix well. Preheat the oven to 170C/350F. Transfer the mixture to an ovenproof dish and bake in the oven for one hour. Allow it to cool before serving.

Spiced Poached Peaches

Ingredients

4 peaches

4 star anise

2 cinnamon sticks

300mls (½ pint) hot water

SERVES 4

44 calories per serving

Method

Place the water, star anise and cinnamon into a saucepan and bring it to the boil. Add the peaches, reduce the heat and simmer gently for 10 minutes. Remove them from the water and serve. You can also add a dollop of crème fraîche or Greek yogurt.

Chocolate Truffle Balls

Ingredients

75g (3oz) peanut butter

25g (1oz) coconut oil

50g (2oz) desiccated (shredded) coconut

25g (1oz) chia seeds

2 teaspoons coconut flour

1 tablespoon 100% cocoa powder

1 tablespoon stevia sweetener

Cocoa powder for coating
(approx. 1 tablespoon)

**MAKES
12**

102
calories
per ball

Method

Place all the ingredients into a bowl or food processor (apart from the cocoa powder for coating) and process until smooth. Using a teaspoon, scoop out a little of the mixture, shape it into a ball and roll it in cocoa powder. Chill before serving.

Tropical Skewers & Fruit Sauce

SERVES 4

167 calories per serving

Ingredients

2 bananas, peeled and thickly sliced

1 pineapple, (approx. 2lb weight) peeled and diced

400g (14oz) strawberries

1 teaspoon 100% cocoa powder or cacao nibs

Method

Place the cocoa powder/cacao nibs and 125g (4oz) of strawberries into a food processor and blitz until creamy. Pour the sauce into a serving bowl. Skewer the bananas, pineapple chunks and remaining strawberries onto skewers. Serve the sauce alongside the skewers.

Blueberry Muffins

Ingredients

250g (9oz) ground almonds (almond flour/almond meal)

150g (5oz) fresh blueberries

3 eggs, whisked

1 teaspoon baking powder

1 teaspoon stevia powder (or to taste)

50mls (2fl oz) melted coconut oil

Pinch of salt

MAKES 10

228 calories each

Method

Lightly grease a 10-hole muffin tin. In a bowl, combine the ground almonds (almond flour/almond meal), baking powder, stevia and salt. In another bowl, combine the coconut oil and eggs then pour the mixture into the dry ingredients. Mix well. Add the blueberries to the mixture and gently stir them in. Spoon some of the mixture into each of the muffin moulds. Transfer them to the oven and bake at 170C/325F for around 20 minutes or until golden.

Warm Berry Compote & Vanilla Cream

Ingredients

250g (9oz) blueberries

250g (9oz) strawberries

100g (3½ oz) redcurrants

100g (3½ oz) blackberries

4 tablespoons double cream, whipped

½ teaspoon vanilla essence

Zest and juice of 1 orange

SERVES 4

139 calories per serving

Method

Place all of the berries into a pan along with the orange zest and juice. Gently heat the berries for around 5 minutes until warmed through. Mix the vanilla essence into the cream. Serve the berries with the cream on top.

Fresh Mango Fool

Ingredients

150g (5oz) fresh mango flesh

100g (3½oz) plain (unflavoured) full-fat yogurt

50g (2oz) crème fraîche

1 passion fruit, halved

Squeeze of lemon juice

SERVES 1

130 calories each

Method

Place the mango into a food processor and process to a purée. In a bowl, whisk together the crème fraîche, lemon juice and yogurt until it thickens. Stir in the mango mixture. Serve into a dessert glass or bowl. Spoon the passion fruit on top and eat straight away.

SNACKS

Low Carb Bread Rolls

Ingredients

100g (4oz) cream cheese

6 eggs

1 teaspoon baking powder

Pinch of salt

MAKES 8

80 calories each

Method

Separate the egg yolks from the whites and place them in two separate bowls. To the egg yolks, add the cream cheese and a pinch of salt, then mix it to a smooth batter. To the egg whites, add the baking powder and whisk them to stiff peaks. Fold the egg yolk mixture into the beaten egg whites and gently combine. Line two baking trays with greaseproof paper. Preheat the oven to 150C/300F. Scoop out a large spoonful of the mixture to form a round bread roll shape. Repeat for the remaining mixture. Transfer them to the oven and cook for 15-20 minutes until the bread is golden. Allow them to cool then store in a plastic bag or an airtight container until ready to use.

Aubergine Fries

Ingredients

125g (4oz) ground almonds (almond meal/almond flour)

1 large egg

1 large aubergine (eggplant, cut lengthwise into batons

1/2 teaspoon salt

1/2 teaspoon ground cumin

1/2 teaspoon paprika

1 tablespoon olive oil

Sea salt

Freshly ground black pepper

SERVES 4

255
calories
each

Method

Place the ground almonds on a large plate and season with salt and pepper. In a bowl, beat the egg and stir in the cumin and paprika and oil. Dip the aubergine batons in egg mixture then roll them in the almond mixture. Place the aubergine on a baking sheet. Transfer it to the oven and cook at 220C/425F for 15 minutes.

Chilli Cheese Chips

Ingredients

100g (3½ oz) Cheddar cheese, grated (shredded)

1 green chilli pepper, de-seeded and thinly sliced

SERVES 4

104 calories each

Method

Line a baking sheet with greaseproof paper. Scoop a tablespoon of the grated (shredded) cheese and place the mound of cheese onto the paper then press it down slightly, keeping a circular shape. Place a thin slice of chilli on top. Repeat for the remaining mixture. Transfer to the oven and cook at 180C/360F for 12 minutes until the cheese has melted. Remove them from the oven and allow them to cool before removing them from the paper.

Baked Aubergine & Garlic Dip

Ingredients

SERVES 4

83 calories each

125g (4oz) plain yogurt

50g (2oz) cucumber, grated (shredded)

2 aubergines (eggplants) cut into slices

1 clove of garlic, crushed

1 tablespoon olive oil

Sea salt

Freshly ground black pepper

Method

Pour the olive oil onto a baking tray and place the aubergine (eggplants) on the tray. Transfer the tray to the oven and cook at 180C/360F for 40 minutes. In the meantime prepare the dip. Combine the yogurt, cucumber and garlic. Season with salt and pepper. Serve the aubergine (eggplant) with a dollop of yogurt.

Tomato & Red Pepper Salsa

Ingredients

4 ripe tomatoes, deseeded and chopped

1 red pepper (bell pepper), finely chopped

4 spring onions (scallions), green part only, finely chopped

Handful of fresh coriander (cilantro) leaves, chopped

Juice of 1 lime

Sea salt

Freshly ground black pepper

SERVES 4

34 calories per serving

Method

Place the red pepper (bell pepper) under a hot grill (broiler) and cook until the skin blisters. Place the pepper in a bowl and cover with plastic wrap for 2 minutes to help bring the skin off and then peel it. Discard the skin and chop the flesh. Combine the pepper in a bowl with the chopped tomatoes, coriander (cilantro) and spring onions. Add the juice of the lime and season with salt and pepper.

Lemon & Ginger Salad Dressing

SERVES 6

128 calories per seving

Ingredients

6 tablespoons extra-virgin olive oil

Juice of 1 lemon

2.5cm (1 inch) chunk of fresh root ginger

1/2 teaspoon mixed herbs

Freshly ground black pepper

Method

Mix all the ingredients together and use as a dressing for salads.

You may also be interested in other titles by
Erin Rose Publishing
which are available in both paperback and ebook.

 Quick Start Guides

SUGAR FREE DIET

SUGAR FREE DIET COOKBOOK

SUGAR FREE FAMILY COOKBOOK

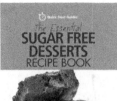 
SUGAR FREE DESSERTS RECIPE BOOK

SUGAR FREE SLOW COOKER Recipe Book

SUGAR FREE DIET Meals For One

BLOOD SUGAR DIET COOKBOOK

BLOOD SUGAR DIET RECIPE BOOK

BLOOD SUGAR DIET 15 Minute Meals

BLOOD SUGAR DIET MEALS FOR ONE

VEGAN RECIPE BOOK For Beginners

THE VEGAN 15 MINUTE COOKBOOK

LOW CARB HIGH FAT DIET

LOW CARB HIGH FAT DIET COOKBOOK

LOW CARB DIET MEALS FOR ONE

GLUTEN-FREE DIET

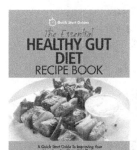

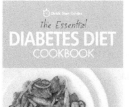
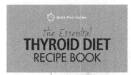

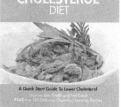

You may also be interested in titles by
Pomegranate Journals

Made in the USA
Monee, IL
20 April 2024

57232769R00063